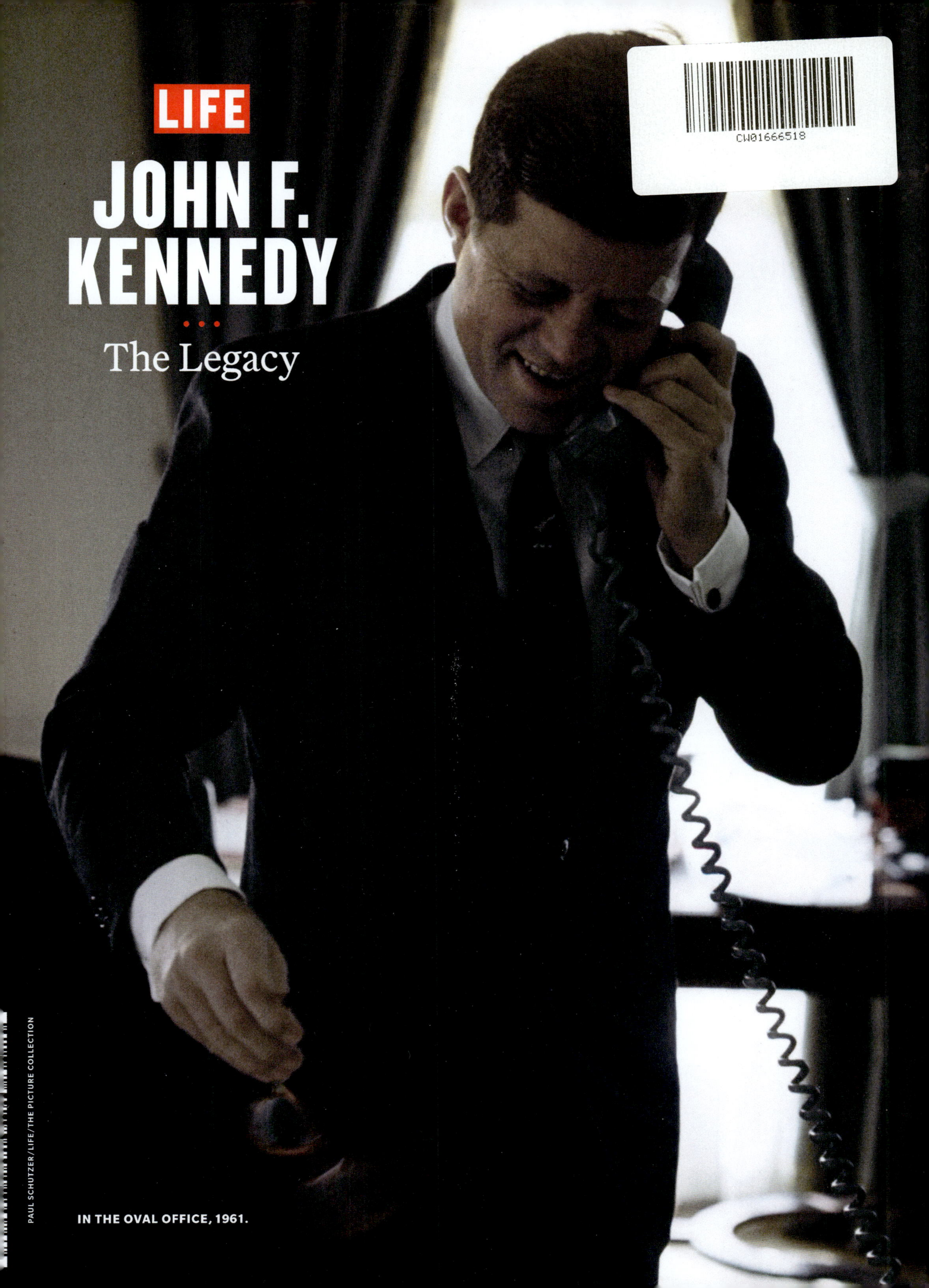

LIFE

JOHN F. KENNEDY

The Legacy

IN THE OVAL OFFICE, 1961.

PAUL SCHUTZER/LIFE/THE PICTURE COLLECTION

CONTENTS

FRONT COVER John F. Kennedy at Hyannis Port, Massachusetts, in 1959. PHOTOGRAPH BY MARK SHAW/MPTVIMAGES

BACK COVER Senator John F. Kennedy and his wife, Jacqueline, campaigning during a ticker-tape parade in Manhattan in June 1960. PHOTOGRAPH BY CORNELL CAPA © INTERNATIONAL CENTER OF PHOTOGRAPHY/MAGNUM

MARK SHAW/MPTVIMAGES

THE FUTURE PRESIDENT in Hyannis Port, Massachusetts, in 1959.

LIFE

WRITER, EDITOR J.I. Baker
DIRECTOR OF PHOTOGRAPHY Christina Lieberman
CREATIVE DIRECTOR Anke Stohlmann/Li'l Robin
COPY CHIEF Parlan McGaw
COPY EDITOR Joel Van Liew
PICTURE EDITOR Rachel Hatch
WRITER-REPORTER Daniel S. Levy
PHOTO ASSISTANT Alessandra Bianco

TIME INC. BOOKS
PUBLISHER Margot Schupf
ASSOCIATE PUBLISHER Allison Devlin
VICE PRESIDENT, FINANCE Terri Lombardi
VICE PRESIDENT, MARKETING Jeremy Biloon
EXECUTIVE DIRECTOR, MARKETING SERVICES Carol Pittard
DIRECTOR, BRAND MARKETING Jean Kennedy
SALES DIRECTOR Christi Crowley
ASSISTANT GENERAL COUNSEL Andrew Goldberg
ASSISTANT DIRECTOR, PRODUCTION Susan Chodakiewicz
SENIOR MANAGER, CATEGORY MARKETING Bryan Christian
BRAND MANAGER Katherine Barnet
PREPRESS MANAGER Alex Voznesenskiy
ASSOCIATE PROJECT AND PRODUCTION MANAGER Anna Riego

EDITORIAL DIRECTOR Kostya Kennedy
CREATIVE DIRECTOR Gary Stewart
DIRECTOR OF PHOTOGRAPHY Christina Lieberman
EDITORIAL OPERATIONS DIRECTOR Jamie Roth Major
SENIOR EDITOR Alyssa Smith
ASSOCIATE ART DIRECTOR Allie Adams
ASSISTANT ART DIRECTOR Anne-Michelle Gallero
COPY CHIEF Rina Bander
ASSISTANT MANAGING EDITOR Gina Scauzillo
ASSISTANT EDITOR Courtney Mifsud

TIME INC. PREMEDIA
Richard K. Prue (Director), Richard Shaffer (Production), Keith Aurelio, Kevin Hart, Rosalie Khan, Patricia Koh, Marco Lau, Brian Mai, Rudi Papiri, Clara Renauro

SPECIAL THANKS Brad Beatson, Melissa Frankenberry, Kristina Jutzi, Simon Keeble, Seniqua Koger, Kate Roncinske, Kristen Zwicker

Published by LIFE BOOKS, an imprint of Time Inc. Books
225 Liberty Street • New York, NY 10281

Vol. 17, No. 8 • April 28, 2017

We welcome your comments and suggestions about LIFE Books. Please write to us at:
LIFE Books, Attention: Book Editors
P.O. Box 62310, Tampa, FL 33662-2310

If you would like to order any of our hardcover Collector's Edition books, please call us at 800-327-6388, Monday through Friday, 7 a.m.–9 p.m. Central Time.

PRESIDENTIAL CANDIDATE John F. Kennedy held his two-year-old daughter, Caroline, on November 1, 1960—a week before he was narrowly elected the 35th President of the United States.

INTRODUCTION

THE BIG IDEA

BY KOSTYA KENNEDY

JOHN F. KENNEDY was born at home, in a three-story Colonial in greater Boston, in late May of 1917, the same springtime in which America entered World War I. He was delivered into one world war and he blossomed into public adulthood during the next, a hero at sea. It may be that no one else born in 1917, or in any year since—oh, well, Elvis maybe—has taken and fulfilled America's imagination as Kennedy did. No one else who represented so handsomely and succinctly the sense of what the country had been and what it might become. He is still the youngest U.S. President ever elected, and still the youngest to die.

Kennedy has been gone for more years than he spent on earth. And yet on the occasion of what, in some incalculably different history, would have been his 100th birthday (his mother, Rose Fitzgerald, lived to 104), he can even now feel enormously present. We have known the stories: the legends and the truths that have shifted and grown and been burnished and chipped over the decades. Raised in a kind of American royal family, groomed for political life. The ascendant career, the dazzling bride, the podium eloquence, the troubles with Cuba, the stand against the Soviets, the drive for civil rights, the other women, the moon, the trip to Dallas in November of 1963.

During his presidency and now in the long aftermath, the Kennedy contradictions have sharpened. Slim and physically compromised—asthmatic as a child, he later fought Addison's disease and colitis, and his chronic back pain sometimes had him on crutches—he was nonetheless the clearest symbol of American robustness and vitality from the moment in his September 26, 1960, debate with Richard Nixon when he looked straight into the television camera and began to speak. Ten words in, Kennedy invoked Abraham Lincoln. Then he spoke about the United States' commitment to freedom and strength and equality, and the individual talents of all Americans. By the time he was done with his opening statement, the art of presidential campaigning, and the nation's image of a leader, would never be the same. "I subscribe completely to the spirit that Senator Kennedy has expressed tonight," Nixon said in his response.

The most enduring of Kennedy's messages tend to be about shortening the distance between people, never about wedging people apart. "*Ich bin ein Berliner,*" he declared in June of 1963 before thousands of assembled Germans and in response to the erecting of the Berlin Wall. *You are one, and I am one with you.* Five months later, on the sunlit afternoon when the presidential motorcade prepared to ride through the crowds at Dealey Plaza, it was Kennedy who insisted that he and Jackie travel with the car's bubble top removed.

Midway through his inaugural address, the speech in which he implored citizens to "ask not what your country can do for you . . . ," Kennedy also said this: "If a free society cannot help the many who are poor, it cannot save the few who are rich."

This was a bedrock notion for Kennedy, who was keenly aware of his privilege, and a bedrock notion for the Kennedy family at large. At the 1992 Democratic National Convention, Ted Kennedy, JFK's younger brother and a long-term senator from Massachusetts, addressed the crowd. "The true test of society is how it treats the least fortunate within it," he said.

And this year, in March, Joseph Patrick Kennedy III, the great-nephew of JFK and a fourth-year congressman, took to a microphone at a House committee meeting to engage in the ongoing battle to provide health care for the poor. It was a battle that Ted had fought for years. "We are judged," Joe III suggested, "not by how we treat the powerful, but by how we care for the least among us."

Perhaps such words would have been spoken in that chamber, in that circumstance, regardless of whether the world had known John F. Kennedy. It's not a unique instinct after all, but it is a surviving one. "A man may die, nations may rise and fall, but an idea lives on," JFK said in '63. And that big idea—of America, even the world, as one people, looking after the weak—is the idea that John F. Kennedy projected, that still clings to him today. ■

PAUL SCHUTZER/LIFE/THE PICTURE COLLECTION

RONNIE PALOGER COLLECTION

IN BOSTON'S CHARLESTOWN neighborhood, at the Bunker Hill Day parade, during his 1946 congressional campaign—"Note hat in JFK's hand," reads a note on the back of this vintage print. "He hated hats."

PORTRAITS OF A YOUNG POLITICIAN

The photos in this gallery are part of a trove of rare JFK memorabilia owned by collector Ronnie Paloger

RONNIE PALOGER COLLECTION

ON HIS HOME TURF in 1952, JFK hobnobbed with fishermen and longshoremen on the Boston docks.

JACKIE AND JACK at their 1953 wedding, which was cannily orchestrated by the Kennedy patriarch, Joseph, as a glamorous, romantic media event.

RONNIE PALOGER COLLECTION

RONNIE PALOGER COLLECTION

JFK IN THE Red Sox dugout, with Tiger slugger Hank Greenberg (right) and Boston's Ted Williams (far left) and Eddie Pellagrini, during his 1946 congressional campaign.

RONNIE PALOGER COLLECTION

JFK IN HIS apartment in Boston's Beacon Hill neighborhood during his 1952 Senate campaign. That's his older brother, Joe, in the photo. The crutches on the floor behind JFK helped him with his chronic back pain.

MOVED

ON JUNE 15, 1946, during JFK's congressional campaign, he spoke at an event for women called "Meet the Kennedys." The attendees, says a description on the back of this rare print, wanted to "fatten him up."

RONNIE PALOGER COLLECTION

CHAPTER ONE

THE RISK-TAKER

After a Japanese destroyer sank his boat, Kennedy braved the elements, the enemy, and the odds

"It was involuntary. They sank my boat."

—JOHN F. KENNEDY

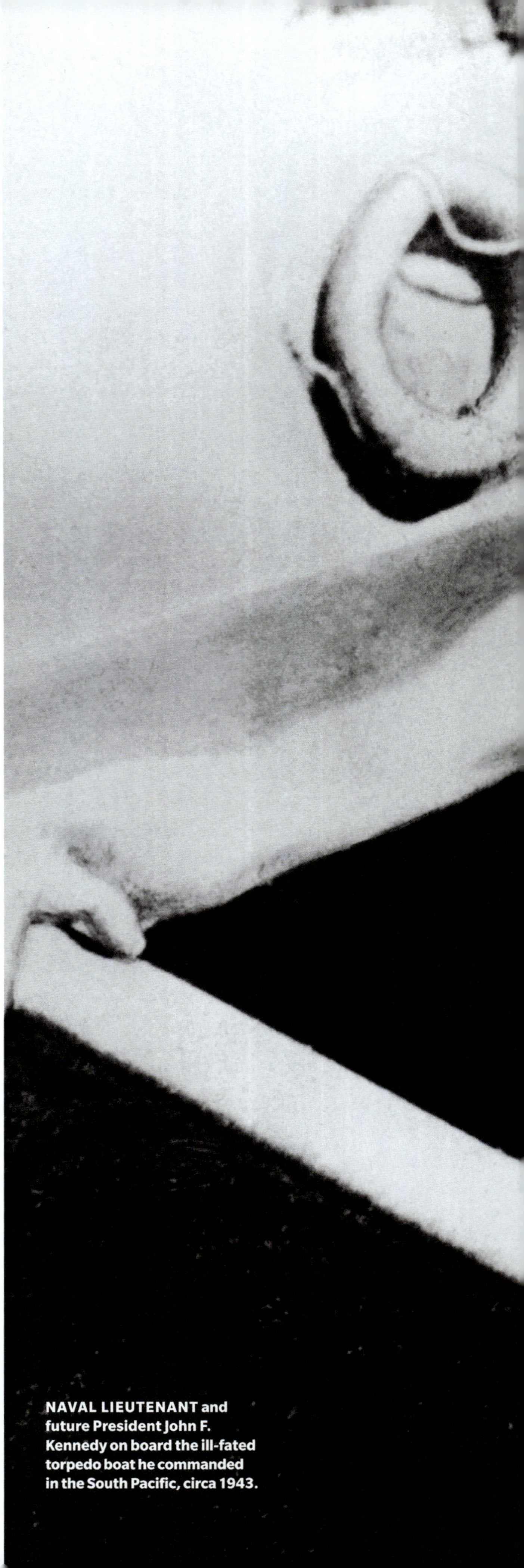

ELLIOTT ERWITT/MAGNUM

NAVAL LIEUTENANT and future President John F. Kennedy on board the ill-fated torpedo boat he commanded in the South Pacific, circa 1943.

D

TEN-YEAR-OLD Jack wearing a football uniform in 1927. The Kennedy boys were raised by their father, Joe, to be fierce competitors, which was hard for young Jack, who was perennially beset by a variety of health problems.

APIC/GETTY

ON AUGUST 2, 1943, a 26-year-old American Navy lieutenant named John F. Kennedy was piloting *PT 109*, one of 15 U.S. Patrol Torpedo boats charged with attacking the Japanese convoys that were helping soldiers in the South Pacific's Solomon Islands. He was cruising a waterway called Blackett Strait, and all was quiet—until 2:30 a.m., when one of his crewmen saw a massive shape looming out of the darkness.

"Ship at two o'clock!" he shouted.

Kennedy looked up to see the Japanese destroyer *Amagiri* heading for his starboard bow. He tried to deploy his torpedoes, but it was too late: The ship sliced the small boat in half, killing two men.

"This is how it feels to be killed," Kennedy thought, lying on the half of the boat that was still afloat, staring up at the destroyer as it left wreckage in its wake. The 10 surviving crew members were scattered around the boat, and burning fuel was flickering on the surface of the water.

"Mr. Kennedy!" someone shouted. "Mr. Kennedy! McMahon is badly hurt."

Jumping from the wreckage, Kennedy swam to the injured man, whose name was Patrick. "How are you, Mac?" he asked.

"I'm all right," he said. "I'm kind of burnt."

This was an understatement. Burns covered the man's face, neck, hands, and feet, and they stung in the salt water. Kennedy towed him to the boat, which was no small feat: Kennedy suffered from debilitating lower back pain, which the collision likely worsened.

At dawn, Kennedy warned his men to keep their heads low to avoid being seen by the Japanese as they waited to be rescued. But U.S. Navy officials thought that *PT 109*'s crew had all perished. When it became clear that no help was on the horizon, Kennedy decided they should swim to an uninhabited coral island—called Plum Pudding—about three and a half miles to the southeast.

Since McMahon couldn't swim, Kennedy towed him, clutching a strap of the burned man's life preserver between his teeth. Whenever Kennedy stopped to catch his breath, he asked, "How do you feel, Mac?"

"I'm okay, Mr. Kennedy," he said. "How about you?"

After swimming for five hours, the men finally arrived at the reef. There was no freshwater on Plum Pudding, according to the JFK presidential library, so when it rained that night, the men licked moisture off the leaves—only to discover the next morning that the foliage was covered with bird droppings.

They renamed the place Bird Island.

Though Kennedy was exhausted and sick, his stomach distended with salt water, he swam a few miles into a nearby passage in search of a U.S. rescue boat. He found none. Worse, he got lost on his way back. As he drifted through the night, he thought that he was yet again near death, but as dawn broke, he discovered that—thanks to the area's circular currents—he was floating near Plum Pudding Island.

After resting on a nearby island, he swam back to Plum Pudding and passed out. On the second day after the crash, with his crew famished and dehydrated, Kennedy decided that they should head to another island, called Olasana. It was larger and therefore more likely to attract Japanese attention, but it was also more likely to offer food.

IRA BLOCK

ELLIOTT ERWITT/MAGNUM

Sure enough, after swimming for three hours (Kennedy towed the fading McMahon again), the crew arrived at the island to find coconuts on the ground. They cracked them open and drank the milk, which made some of them sick.

The men were steadily weakening, some suffering from coral cuts—and McMahon's burns had begun to rot—so Kennedy kept searching for a way out. He and Ensign George Ross found a box of Japanese candy on a nearby island. The sugar helped allay their hunger but also raised the question: Was the enemy near? After encountering natives who served as Allied scouts and had access to a boat, Kennedy dispatched them to an Allied post with a message he had scratched on a coconut husk, reading in part "11 alive... need small boat... Kennedy."

On the fifth day, the islanders returned, and brought Kennedy to the post. Soon, a PT boat showed up to take him back to rescue his crew. "Hey, Jack!" someone shouted from the approaching vessel.

"Where the hell you been?" Kennedy replied.

"We got some food for you."

"No thanks," the young lieutenant wryly said. "I just had a coconut."

"COURAGE," ROBERT F. Kennedy wrote in 1963, a month after his brother's assassination, "is the virtue that President Kennedy most admired. He sought out those people who had demonstrated in some way, whether it was on a battlefield or a baseball diamond, in a speech or fighting for a cause, that they had courage, that they would stand up, that they could

CONTINUED ON PAGE 27

A SOLOMON ISLANDER (top) with a dugout canoe at the tiny island, now named for Kennedy, where the *PT 109* crew first struggled ashore after the destruction of their boat. Bottom: A rare (and damaged) photo of *PT 109* taken in the Solomon islands. Opposite: Kennedy examined the coconut on which he had scratched a message that led to the rescue of his men.

JOHN F. KENNEDY PRESIDENTIAL LIBRARY AND MUSEUM, BOSTON

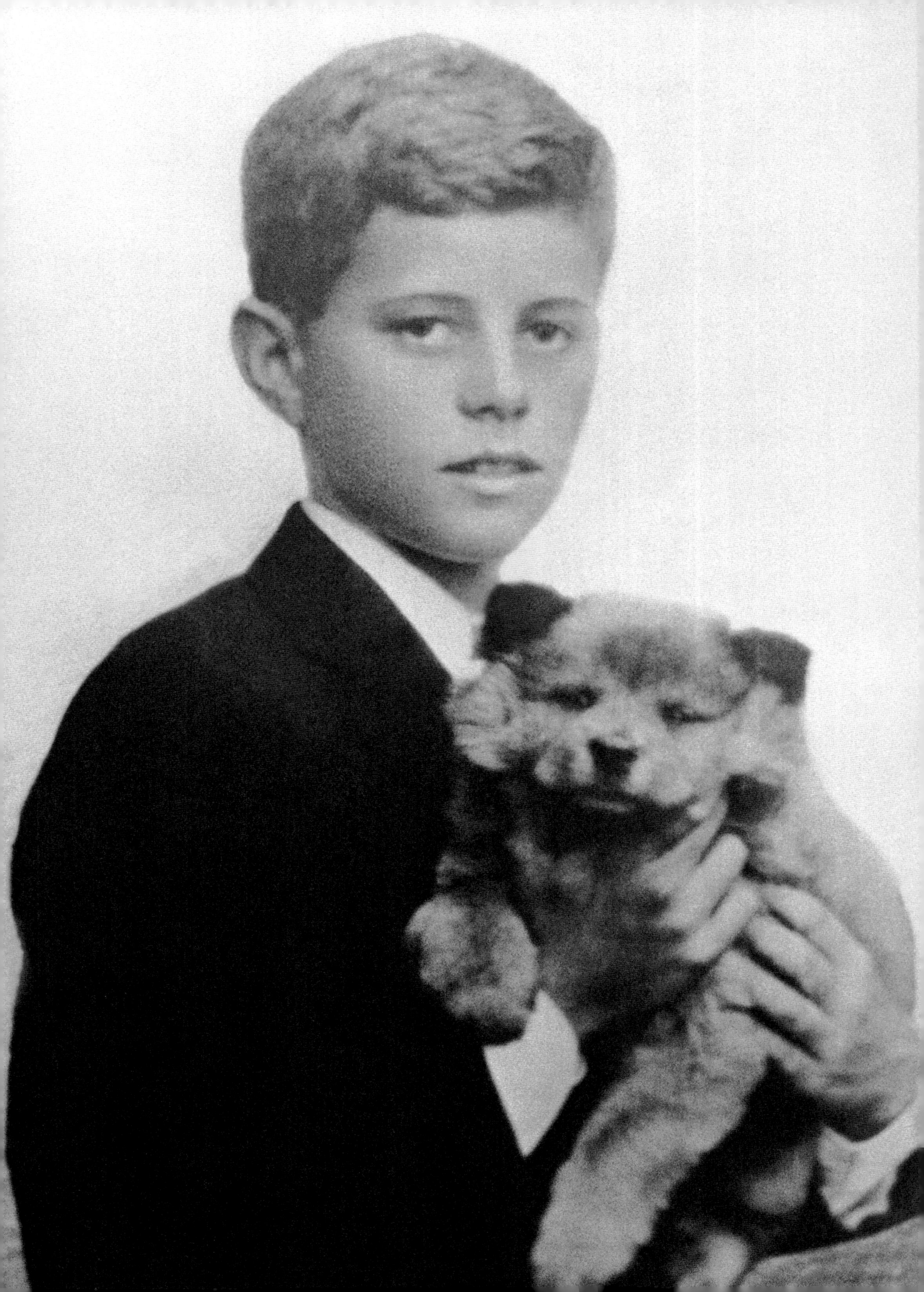

RONNIE PALOGER COLLECTION

MAGNUM COLLECTION/MAGNUM

ELLIOTT ERWITT/MAGNUM

PORTRAIT OF THE President as a young man (opposite). Top: Kennedy and his Choate classmate Ralph "Rip" Horton rehearsed a scene for the drama club. Bottom: Kennedy danced with his sister Eunice at her 18th birthday party, held at the London residence of their father, who was then the American ambassador to Great Britain.

CONTINUED FROM PAGE 22
be counted on."

These words were part of a new foreword to JFK's Pulitzer Prize–winning book, *Profiles in Courage,* which he had written while recovering from near-fatal back surgery in 1954—partly the result of the injury he'd sustained in the South Pacific. In the book, Kennedy profiled American icons such as Daniel Webster, Thomas Hart Benton, and Sam Houston. He also quoted Ernest Hemingway to the effect that courage is "grace under pressure."

Kennedy's own grace stemmed in part from his lifelong confrontation with mortality. From a perilously early age, he had battled stomach problems, unexplained allergies, severe back trouble, and Addison's disease, a disorder affecting the adrenal glands. "At least one half of the days that he spent on this earth were days of intense physical pain," Bobby continued. "When we were growing up together we used to laugh about the great risk a mosquito took in biting Jack Kennedy—with some of his blood the mosquito was almost sure to die."

It wasn't easy to be sickly in the Kennedy clan. Yes, the children were raised in a privileged world of servants and limousines, seaside houses and horseback riding on Cape Cod, but it was not a world of indulgence. The family's ruthless patriarch, Joseph, had made multiple fortunes on Wall Street and in Hollywood, and he instilled in all his children—particularly the boys—a fierce competitiveness that turned even games into a kind of juvenile warfare. He also insisted on stoicism: "Kennedys don't cry," he told them. Sure, he loved his kids, but he intended to use them—particularly his eldest, Joseph Jr.—to

THE KENNEDY FAMILY at their compound in Hyannis Port, Massachusetts, in the 1930s. Seated, from left: Patricia, Robert, matriarch Rose, John, and patriarch Joseph Sr., with Edward on his lap. Standing, from left: Joseph Jr., Kathleen, Rosemary, Jean, and Eunice (rear, in polka dots).

BACHRACH/GETTY

GAMMA-KEYSTONE/GETTY

fulfill the political ambitions that he himself had never achieved. From a very early age, JFK knew that he had to overcome his weaknesses.

But the flip side of his courage was recklessness, which was particularly apparent in his compulsive womanizing. His eventual paramours allegedly included a suspected East German spy, Marilyn Monroe, and a mistress that he shared with a Mafia boss (more on that later).

After graduating from Harvard in June 1940, JFK tried to join the Navy but was rejected because of his health. So his powerful father pulled strings, which was, ultimately, how JFK got the chance to become a hero in the South Pacific.

The reality behind the *PT 109* story is more complex than the legend might suggest. Though JFK undeniably showed bravery after the crash, a Navy inquiry found evidence of poor seamanship. Kennedy himself thought he would be court-martialed when he returned to the base. Even his older brother, Joe, questioned his behavior. "What I really want to know," he scolded, "is where the hell were you when the destroyer hove into sight, and exactly what were your moves?"

Despite the skepticism, JFK was awarded the prestigious Navy and Marine Corps Medal (for "extremely heroic conduct" and "courage, endurance, and excellent leadership") along with the Purple Heart, which reflected the injuries he had sustained in the ordeal. Kennedy, for his part, was characteristically self-effacing: "It was involuntary," he said. "They sank my boat."

The *PT 109* incident marked the point at which Kennedy the mortal man first merged with myth. The

KENNEDY IN HIS U.S. Navy uniform, circa 1940 (opposite). His older brother, Lieutenant Joseph Kennedy Jr. (above), in an airplane cockpit during World War II.

FRANK TURGENT/HULTON/GETTY

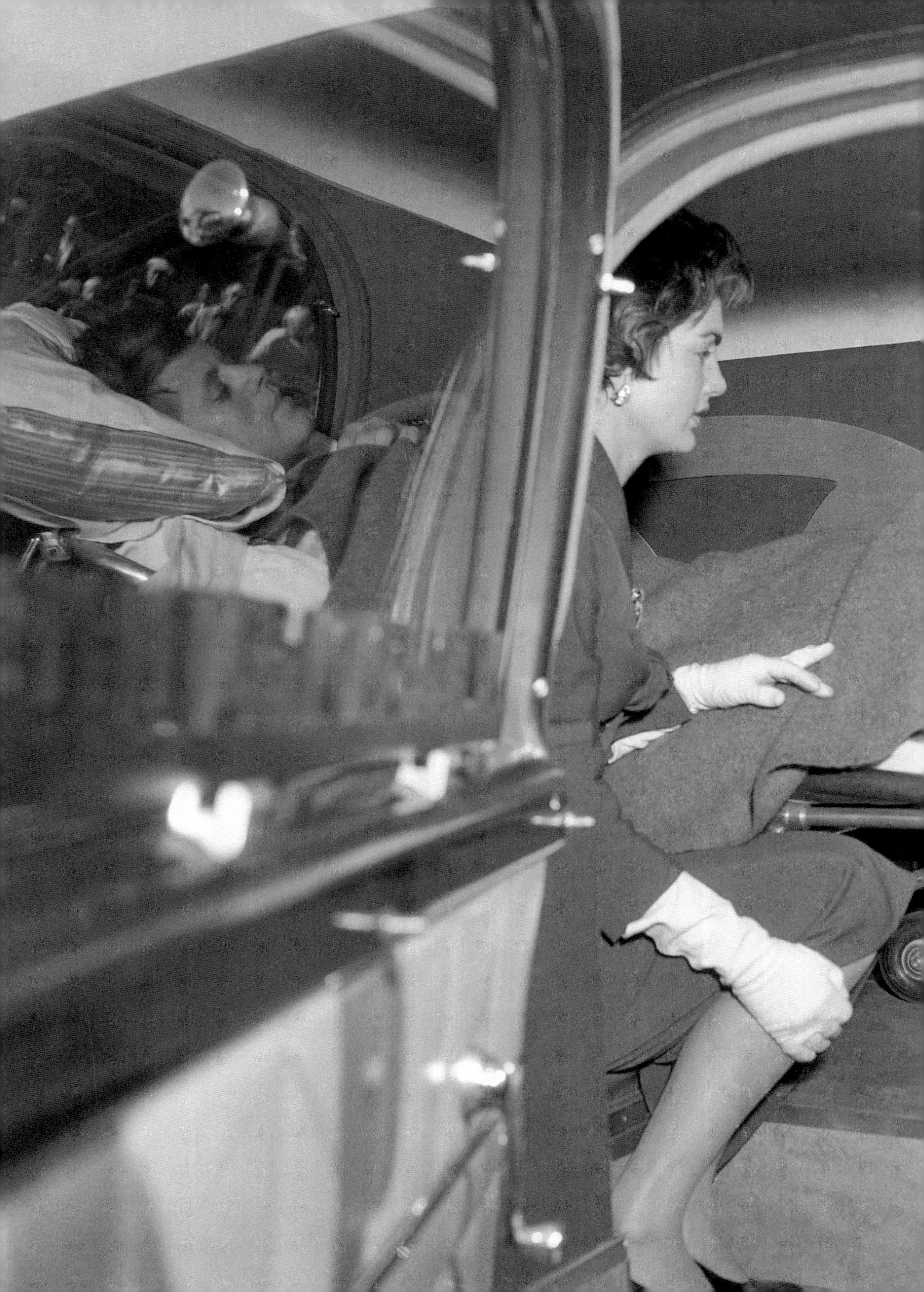

cultural canonization began with novelist John Hersey's "Survival," a story about the disaster that appeared in the June 17, 1944, issue of the *New Yorker*. Father Joe, aware that the *New Yorker* had an elite and limited readership, arranged to have a condensed version published in the vastly more popular *Reader's Digest*.

The disaster in the South Pacific may have indirectly led to JFK's presidency. Jealous of his younger brother's accomplishment, Joe Jr. tried to outshine him by "volunteering for riskier and riskier missions even after he was supposed to come home," according to journalist Vince Bzdek. The eldest Kennedy son paid the ultimate price for his bravado: On August 12, 1944, Joe Jr. was flying a dangerous mission in an experimental plane containing 10 tons of high explosives that detonated in midair. (It was possibly caused by a faulty bomb-arming mechanism.)

"Now the burden falls on me," JFK told a friend after the tragedy. Though he had initially considered becoming a teacher or a writer, he knew what was expected of him. "It was like being drafted," he later told a journalist. "My father wanted his oldest son in politics. 'Wanted' isn't the right word. He demanded it."

The Kennedy political machine went into motion. In 1946, JFK ran as a Democrat for Congress in Massachusetts's 11th congressional district and won. (Joseph distributed tens of thousands of copies of the *Reader's Digest PT 109* story to voters in key election neighborhoods.) He served six years in the House of Representatives and in 1952 was elected to the U.S. Senate, where he served until 1960. But John—or, rather, Joe—was hardly finished.

The White House beckoned. ■

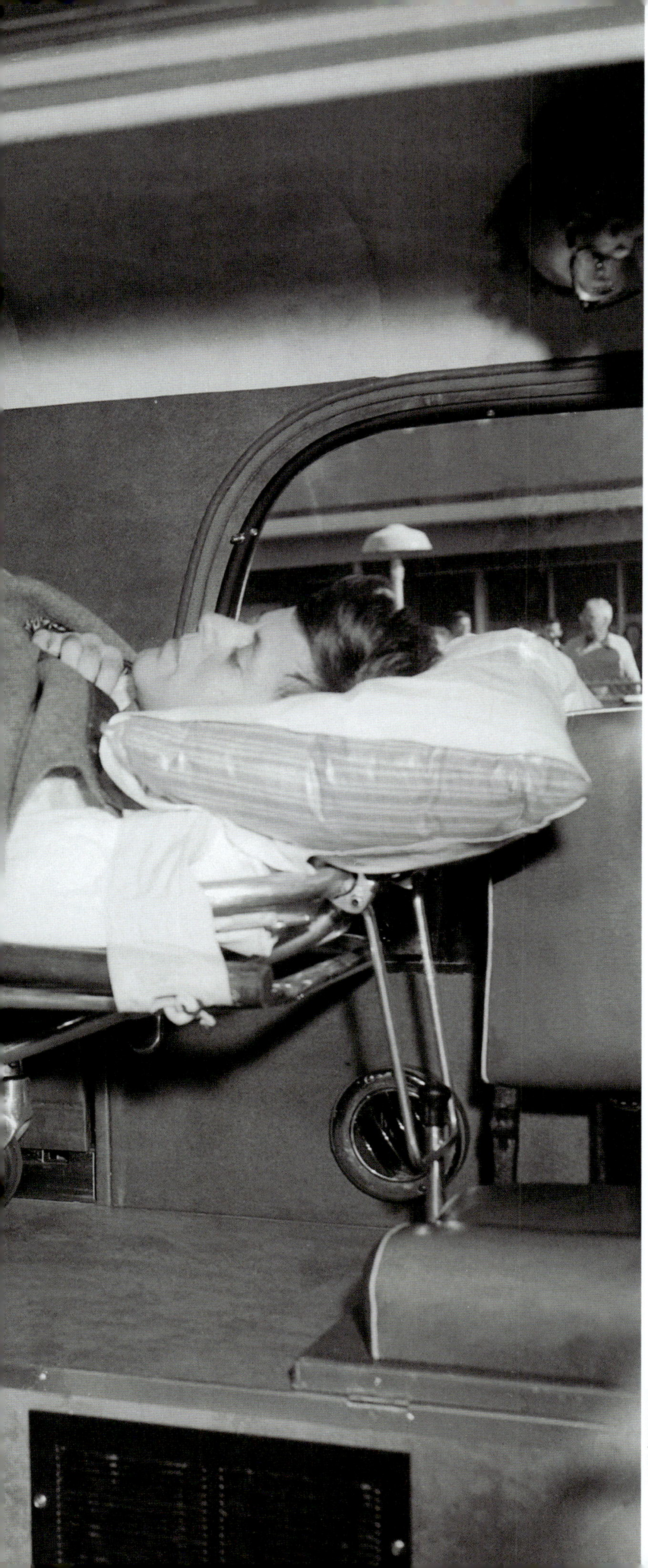

BETTMANN/GETTY

ACCOMPANIED BY his wife, Jacqueline, a perilously ill Senator Kennedy was taken by ambulance to his father's residence in Palm Beach, Florida, following the surgery in New York that almost killed him, in 1954.

CHAPTER TWO

THE TV STAR

Kennedy used the new medium of television to enter American living rooms ... and hearts

"Political shows, like quiz shows, can be fixed—and sometimes are."

—JOHN F. KENNEDY

BETTMANN/GETTY

THE PRESIDENT just before a television broadcast on July 3, 1963.

ON SEPTEMBER 26, 1960, Vice President Richard M. Nixon was on his way to face JFK in the first-ever televised presidential debate when he banged his knee climbing from a car in downtown Chicago. It was the latest blow for the seasoned politician. The previous month, Nixon had hurt the same knee on a car door while campaigning in North Carolina, resulting in an infection that put him in the hospital. He was still running a fever during the debate.

Nevertheless, Nixon remained the odds-on favorite to win the presidency. He had been Dwight D. Eisenhower's Vice President for eight years following an influential career in Congress, while his 43-year-old Catholic opponent, Kennedy, had failed to distinguish himself in either the House or the Senate. Nixon's most frequent accusation against Kennedy was that he lacked the gravitas and experience to be President at a time when the nation was threatened by the cold war, Fidel Castro's Cuba, and civil rights unrest.

But Nixon underestimated the new medium of television, while Kennedy instinctively understood that its power stemmed not from words or ideas but from image. His father had worked in Hollywood, after all, and his mother, Rose, was the daughter of John Francis Fitzgerald, the mayor of Boston and a prominent congressman. "Appearance was very important to her," Dr. Barbara A. Perry, director of presidential studies at the University of Virginia Miller Center, tells LIFE. "She was a Victorian perfectionist who always wanted the family to be perfect. It was as basic and as simple as their teeth. They weren't born with their dazzling smiles—she was getting them all to an orthodontist when most people didn't know that was a possibility."

Joseph's ambition and Rose's perfectionism combined with the influence of British royalty, with whom the Kennedy family had hobnobbed during the late 1930s and 1940, when Joseph was the U.S. ambassador to the United Kingdom. "They were going to Buckingham Palace and Windsor for weekends," says Perry. "The girls had debutante balls and coming-out parties, and the eldest daughter, Kathleen, married a British nobleman. They were bringing the family out from the peat bogs—just two generations since Rose's forebears had moved from Ireland!"

In 1952, at a Georgetown dinner party, JFK met a beautiful debutante named Jacqueline Lee Bouvier. Born the daughter of a wealthy Catholic stockbroker in 1929, Jackie was "a darling child," according to one of her teachers, "the prettiest little girl, very clever, very artistic, and full of the devil."

In 1951, having graduated from George Washington University, she was working as "the Inquiring Camera Girl" for a Washington, D.C., newspaper when she met John. "I think I'm in love," she wrote to a Catholic priest, adding that JFK was "like Macbeth" in his ambitions. "Maybe I'm just dazzled and picture myself in a glittering world of crowned heads and Men of Destiny and not just a sad little housewife."

On September 12, 1953, the couple married in Newport, Rhode Island—an event that, thanks to Joseph, became a grand attention-grabbing extravaganza. "Joe knew that this kind of event made great copy in LIFE magazine," says Perry, "so he pulled out all the stops. Even then, he had

CONTINUED ON PAGE 38

KENNEDY DURING **his presidential campaign, which changed politics forever by emphasizing the relatively inexperienced young man's youth and good looks.**

PAUL SCHUTZER/LIFE/THE PICTURE COLLECTION

LISA LARSEN/LIFE/THE PICTURE COLLECTION

JFK AND HIS new bride, Jacqueline, sitting down to fruit cup in pineapple bowls at their wedding reception in Newport, Rhode Island, on September 12, 1953.

HY PESKIN/GETTY

CONTINUED FROM PAGE 34

his eyes trained on the White House."

Which brings us back to the debate of September 26, 1960—the first of four. That night, instead of the preempted *Andy Griffith Show,* a rapt nation watched Kennedy coolly face the cameras looking tan, confident, and handsome. Nixon, on the other hand, looked shifty, pale, and tired. A last-minute coat of Lazy Shave, a makeup designed to hide the older man's perennial five-o'clock shadow, melted in the TV lights, causing beads of perspiration to appear on his slack jowls.

"The difference was telling," wrote Robert Dallek in his Kennedy biography, *An Unfinished Life.* "Kennedy came across as a leader who intended to deal with the nation's greatest problems; Nixon registered with voters as someone trying to gain an advantage over an adversary." Henry Cabot Lodge, Nixon's running mate, was more succinct. Watching from a hotel in Texas, he said to an aide: "That son of a bitch just lost the election."

Nixon performed better in the subsequent debates, but the damage had been done. Less than two months later, Kennedy beat Nixon by 112,827 votes—largely thanks to the debates.

"THE WORLD of entertainment—show-biz, if you please—has become the Sixth Estate, just as Hawaii became the 50th state," said Bette Davis at

CONTINUED ON PAGE 43

JACKIE AND JACK (above) sharing a rare vacation at the Kennedy compound in Hyannis Port, Massachusetts, in June 1953. Opposite: Campaigning for the nation's highest office in 1960.

CORNELL CAPA © INTERNATIONAL CENTER OF PHOTOGRAPHY/MAGNUM

KENNEDY

PAUL SCHUTZER/LIFE/THE PICTURE COLLECTION

JACKIE WATCHED anxiously as her husband and Republican rival Richard Nixon debated on October 13, 1960, in New York City.

HANK WALKER/LIFE/THE PICTURE COLLECTION

BUD GRAY/MPTVIMAGES

NATIONAL ARCHIVES/THE PICTURE COLLECTION, INC.

KENNEDY MADE a point as Nixon wiped away sweat during their second debate, on October 7 (opposite, top). For the first time in history, the nation could watch the presidential debates on TV (bottom). Above right: The candidate and his soon-to-be First Lady on the set of a West Virginia TV show in April 1960.

CONTINUED FROM PAGE 38

the ball held at the National Guard Armory on January 19, 1961, the eve of JFK's inauguration. Kennedy had asked his friend Frank Sinatra to produce the event, and the singer pulled out all the stops, calling on the best of the entertainment world: Mahalia Jackson, Harry Belafonte, Jimmy Durante, and Ethel Merman, among many others.

The whole shebang was, according to a young *Washington Post* reporter named Tom Wolfe, "a gilt-edged, mink-lined, silk-hatted, 10-gallon, 100-proof" celebration that perfectly exemplified the administration's youthful new image. It was, as Davis had suggested, the first manifestation of the administration's mix of politics and Hollywood-style glamour. JFK, for one, knew how to exploit it. On the way to the armory that night, he told his limo driver to turn on the interior lights, so that everyone could see how stunning Jackie looked in her silvery silk dress.

The event wasn't televised, but the following day's inauguration brought the world its first formal taste of the Kennedy style. "JFK looked every bit the well-dressed man, and he knew that this would contrast with the big suits and frumpy hats of the Eisenhower and Truman 1950s," says Perry. Even though it was cold, Kennedy removed his overcoat, showing off his slick suit, and Jackie—in sharp contrast to the matronly women around her—had been dressed by Oleg Cassini, a former Hollywood wardrobe designer, in a fawn-colored coat and her trademark pillbox hat.

Five days after the inauguration, Kennedy appeared in the first-ever televised presidential press conference. At the time, "there were only three or four newspapers in the entire United States that carried a full transcript of a presidential press conference," according to his press secretary, Pierre Salinger. "Therefore, what people read was a distillation... We thought that they should have the opportunity to see it in full."

Though Kennedy almost single-handedly created the cult of personality in American politics, he warned against the dangers of its growing influence. "It is in your power to perceive deception, to shut off gimmickry, to reward honesty, to demand legislation where needed," he wrote in—of all places—*TV Guide* in 1959. "Without your approval, no TV show is worthwhile and no politician can exist." In the wrong hands, Kennedy added, television could be used for "manipulation, exploitation, and gimmicks. It can be abused by demagogues, by appeals to emotions and prejudice and ignorance."

Nearly 60 years later, his admonition remains as relevant as ever. ■

DENNIS STOCK/MAGNUM

PAUL SCHUTZER/LIFE/THE PICTURE COLLECTION (2)

JACKIE AND JFK (opposite) left their Georgetown home on their way to the presidential pre-inaugural ball at the National Guard Armory in Washington, on January 19, 1961. Top: Frank Sinatra was in charge of the event. Bottom: The soon-to-be First Couple walked to the inauguration.

CHAPTER THREE

THE SPACE PIONEER

• • •

Fulfilling Kennedy's dream, the United States reached the moon before the end of the 1960s

"We choose to go to the moon."

—JOHN F. KENNEDY, SEPTEMBER 12, 1962

BETTMANN/GETTY

WEARING THE NASA Distinguished Service Medal presented to him by the President, astronaut John Glenn showed Kennedy and Vice President Lyndon Johnson *Friendship 7*, the space capsule that carried him out of the earth's orbit.

NASA

THE MEN selected for Project Mercury, the first American manned space program, at Virginia's Langley Air Force Base in 1959. From left: Alan Shepard, Scott Carpenter, L. Gordon Cooper, Donald Slayton, Virgil Grissom, John Glenn, and Walter Schirra.

RALPH MORSE/LIFE/THE PICTURE COLLECTION

On May 25, 1961, Kennedy promised Americans the moon—literally. "I believe that this nation should commit itself to achieving the goal, before this decade is out, of landing a man on the moon and returning him safely to the earth," he told a joint session of Congress.

The speech swiftly spurred an 89 percent increase in NASA's budget, which rose by an additional 101 percent the following year. But the President's motivations weren't entirely idealistic. He desperately needed a "win" in the midst of what columnist George Will, in 2011, would call "the most incompetent first year of any presidency."

In 1957, the Soviets had successfully launched Sputnik, the first artificial earth satellite, which both threatened and embarrassed the United States. In response, President Dwight D. Eisenhower created the National Aeronautics and Space Administration and launched Project Mercury, the United States' first man-in-space program, selecting seven men to serve as astronauts.

But the Soviets remained in the lead. In April 1961, mere months after JFK's inauguration, the United States was embarrassed once again when Soviet cosmonaut Yuri Gagarin became the first man to travel into space and orbit the earth. At the same time, Kennedy faced more serious and ever-increasing trouble closer to home: Believing that Cuba's communist dictator, Fidel Castro, could bring communism to the Western Hemisphere, the Kennedy administration tried to topple his regime with April 1961's Bay of Pigs invasion. It failed miserably, becoming a political, military, and public relations fiasco.

To offset all that, the President needed a success. He found it when, on May 5, 1961, Project Mercury astronaut Alan Shepard completed a 15-minute 22-second suborbital flight, becoming the first American in space.

Three days after the historic flight, Kennedy awarded Shepard the NASA Distinguished Service Medal in Washington, D.C. "This flight was made out in the open with all the possibilities of failure, which would have been damaging to our country's prestige," Kennedy announced. "Because great risks were taken in that regard, it seems to me that we have some right to claim that this open society of ours which risked much, gained much." A subsequent parade in Shepard's honor attracted what LIFE called "one of the biggest crowds in Washington history."

Kennedy had hitched his reputation to the stars, but the truth is that he had never been an advocate of space exploration. In the 1950s, while still a senator, he and his brother Bobby had dinner with MIT professor Charles Draper, according to Richard Collin in *John F. Kennedy: History, Memory, Legacy*. The Kennedys, Draper said, "could not be convinced that all rockets were not a waste of money and space navigation even worse."

As late as 1962, JFK told NASA administrator James Webb that a moon-landing goal was risky, since failure would be embarrassing. Webb responded that exploring space wasn't just about a time line—there were scientific and technological advantages involved. JFK disagreed. "This is, whether we like it or not, a race," he said. "Everything we do [in space] ought to be tied into getting to the moon ahead of the Russians . . . Otherwise, we shouldn't be spending

CONTINUED ON PAGE 52

MR 7

UNITED STATES ARMY/THE NEW YORK TIMES/REDUX

JOSEPH SCHERSCHEL/LIFE/THE PICTURE COLLECTION

RALPH MORSE/LIFE/THE PICTURE COLLECTION

ABOUT TO BECOME the first American in space, Shepard (opposite) sprinted toward the launchpad at Florida's Cape Canaveral on May 5, 1961. Top: Kennedy and the First Lady watched Shepard's flight with (from left) Johnson, aide Arthur Schlesinger Jr., and Admiral Arleigh Burke. Bottom: Kennedy pinned the NASA Distinguished Service Medal on Shepard's lapel.

ROBERT KNUDSEN/WHITE HOUSE/JOHN F. KENNEDY PRESIDENTIAL LIBRARY AND MUSEUM, BOSTON

CONTINUED FROM PAGE 49

this kind of money, because I'm not that interested in space."

But his perspective kept changing. On February 20, 1962, Marine Corps lieutenant colonel John H. Glenn made history when he became the first American to orbit the earth. During the four-hour 55-minute 23-second flight, Glenn saw three sunsets and sunrises, returning to earth as "the last true national hero America has ever had," according to Tom Wolfe, author of *The Right Stuff.* Though America still lagged behind the Soviets, "John Glenn made us whole again!" Wolfe wrote. The country was catching up to the Soviets—and Kennedy's ambitions were growing.

On September 12, 1962, the President gave one of his most inspiring speeches at Rice University in Houston, Texas. "We choose to go to the moon in this decade and do the other things, not because they are easy, but because they are hard," he said.

The nation embraced the challenge. The following May, astronaut Gordon Cooper orbited earth 22 times over the course of 34 hours and 20 minutes—a record for a manned space flight and the first American extraterrestrial effort to overshadow the Soviets.

The United States was on its way to the moon. ■

"WE CHOOSE to go to the moon," Kennedy said in his historic speech at Rice University on September 12, 1962, above. Opposite: Rocket scientist and former Nazi Wernher von Braun showed Kennedy and Johnson the Saturn C-1 booster rocket at the George C. Marshall Space Flight Center in Huntsville, Alabama, in 1962.

BOB GOMEL/THE LIFE IMAGES COLLECTION/GETTY

BETTMANN/GETTY

KENNEDY AND GLENN at a victory parade in Cocoa Beach, Florida, just after the astronaut made history by becoming the first American to orbit the earth.

CHAPTER FOUR

THE FIRST FATHER

• • •

Though Kennedy wasn't always good to Jackie, he was a deeply devoted dad

CECIL STOUGHTON/WHITE HOUSE/JOHN F. KENNEDY PRESIDENTIAL LIBRARY AND MUSEUM, BOSTON

"He loved those children."

—JACQUELINE KENNEDY, 1964

KENNEDY IN THE Oval Office with daughter Caroline and son John (also known as John-John) in October 1962.

KENNEDY WORKED while John-John played in the Oval Office's *Resolute* desk. Published after JFK's assassination, this image fueled the public's conflation of the President's death with the loss of the nation's hopes and dreams.

ESTATE OF STANLEY TRETICK LLC/CORBIS/GETTY

NEARLY EVERY morning in the White House, John F. Kennedy devoured news and briefings along with his breakfast—eggs, bacon, and toast—in bed. He was often joined by his two children: Caroline, born in 1957, and John Jr., who had been born eight weeks before the 1961 inauguration.

They were the youngest children of a sitting President since Theodore Roosevelt's. "Kennedy would exercise with them on the pale carpet, getting them to touch their toes, imitating the popular morning television exercise man, Jack LaLanne," the journalist Andrew Cohen wrote in *Two Days in June.* According to Jackie, "He loved those children tumbling around him in this sort of—sensual is the only way I can think of it."

Jackie mostly tried to shield the children from the public eye, but they were a crucial part of the new administration's image. "There was this sense of possibility and youth and activity in the Kennedy White House—they had such a big, active family," says Barbara Perry. The children had a tree house on the White House lawn, a preschool, and a swimming pool. They also had a menagerie complete with horses, dogs (including Pushinka, the offspring of a dog from the Russian space program—a gift from Soviet premier Nikita Khrushchev—and Pushinka's puppies), a cat, a canary, parakeets, hamsters, and a rabbit named Zsa Zsa.

Yet the family's charmed life did not seem entirely out of reach. The Kennedys were American royalty, yes, but they nevertheless reflected the collective hope, optimism, and ambition characteristic of "the Greatest Generation," which had emerged in the wake of the Second World War. This was also the era of the baby boom, a fertile trend reflected by this fresh young couple and their children.

Despite her sophistication and beauty, Jackie was eminently relatable—perhaps because of her demure, soft-spoken shyness. At 31, she was the third youngest First Lady ever, and her predecessors were Bess Truman and Mamie Eisenhower. "They were both in their sixties when they left the White House, and they were grandmotherly, not stylish," says Perry. "Then here comes Mrs. Kennedy, at 31, looking like everyone's older sister or cousin, and she has a newborn and a toddler who are cute as buttons—and they just keep getting cuter as days go by."

Jackie was also instrumental in bringing attention to the arts and sciences, inviting creative figures such as choreographer George Balanchine and composer Igor Stravinsky to teas and to elaborate French dinners in the nation's capital. On February 14, 1962, she opened the White House doors to television viewers across the world—including in Russia and China—turning a previously unseen political fortress into something like the nation's home.

Having funded a $2 million dollar renovation through private donations, Jackie showed 80 million viewers the stateroom ("The china is the Eisenhower gold," she said), the Red Room ("Everything in this room is Empire"), the Blue Room ("The view from here is so pretty—you can see the Washington Monument"), and the Lincoln bedroom ("One of Andrew Jackson's magnolia trees is right outside the window"). "I just think that everything in the White House should be the best," she said—and the nation agreed.

Later, of course, cracks in the Kennedy marriage emerged. Like his father and brothers, JFK was revealed as an unapologetic serial philanderer. ("This administration is going to do for sex what the previous one did for golf," one aide said.)

He was also a cool customer who kept his emotions to himself. "I would describe Jack as rather like me in that his life is an iceberg," Jackie once wrote. "The public life is above the water—& the private life—is submerged . . . I'd say Jack didn't want to reveal himself at all." (When Jack once offered her "a penny for your thoughts," she responded, "If I told them to you, they wouldn't be mine, would they?") Jack and Jackie were, according to one friend, "the two most isolated, most alone people I ever met."

But in the summer of 1963, tragedy bonded them. Pregnant with a son they planned to call Patrick, Jackie was relaxing under doctor's orders on Cape Cod, having already suffered a miscarriage. She had also delivered a stillborn daughter, Arabella, in 1956, while Jack was cavorting in Capri with a handful of young women. On August 7, 1963, the First Lady was taking John Jr. and Caroline to horseback-riding lessons when she was overcome with back and stomach pains.

She had, as it turned out, gone into labor six weeks early. Whisked from the White House via helicopter, a stricken JFK muttered, "I'm never there when she needs me." The tiny boy was diagnosed with a respiratory syndrome and lived only 39 hours. "He put up quite a fight," said the grieving President, who was holding the boy's fingers when he died. "He was a beautiful baby."

The man who had been taught that "Kennedys don't cry" began, at

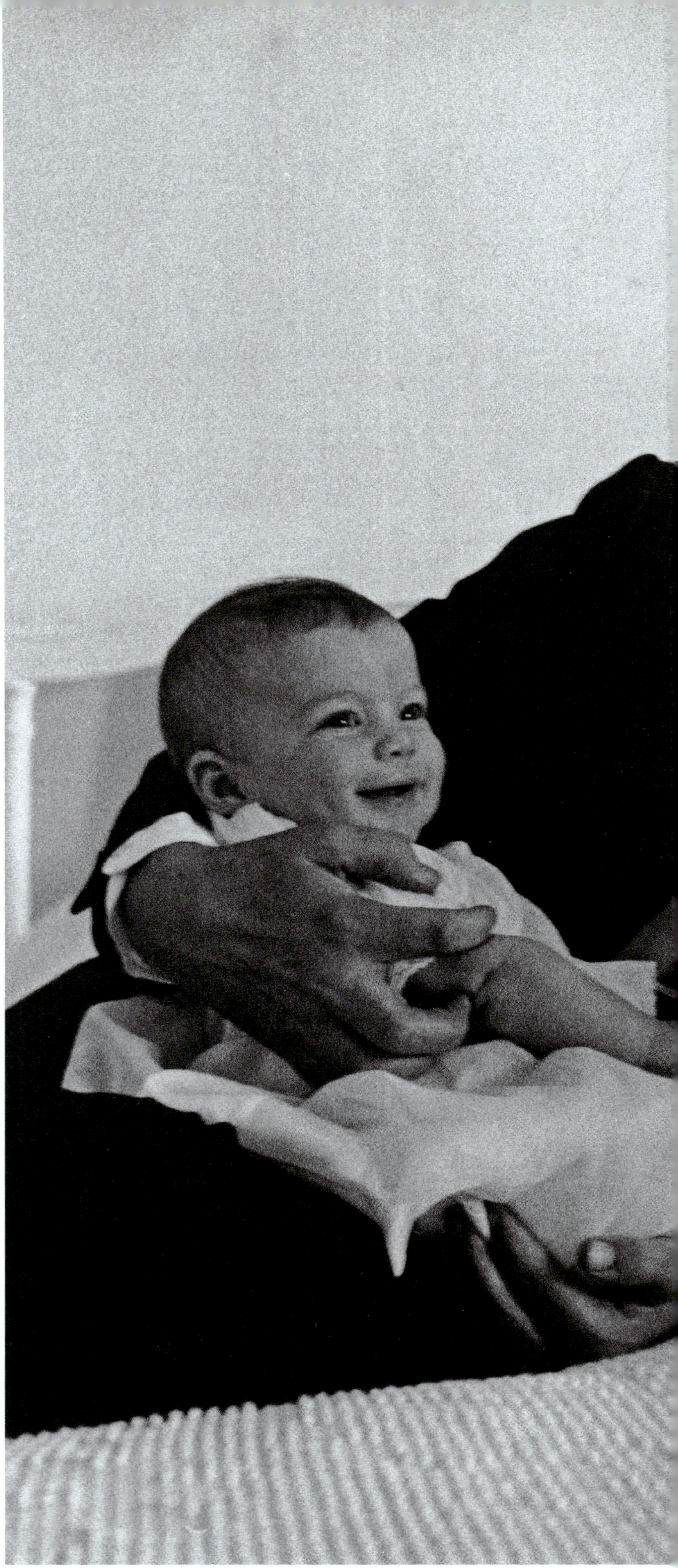

ED CLARK/LIFE/THE PICTURE COLLECTION

SENATOR KENNEDY and Jackie at home with Caroline in Georgetown, Washington, D.C., in March 1958.

ALFRED EISENSTAEDT/LIFE/THE PICTURE COLLECTION

PHOTOQUEST/GETTY

ESTATE OF STANLEY TRETICK LLC/CORBIS/GETTY

JFK WITH CAROLINE (opposite, top) circa August 1960. Bottom: John-John was thrilled by the gift of a toy parrot from the President. Above: Kennedy and kids played with the pony Macaroni in June 1962.

last, to cry—and the "iceberg" began to thaw as the President revealed a newfound affection for and commitment to his wife. He may even have resolved to curb his infidelities, according to a White House intern he had been seeing for a year—and Jackie must have felt this change.

"There's just one thing I couldn't stand," Jackie said in the hospital, "if I ever lost you."

Though Jackie was too weak to attend the funeral in Boston, Jack sat, weeping openly, in the front row of Cardinal Cushing's private chapel. Later, the President took a money clip made from a gold St. Christopher medal—a wedding gift from Jackie—and put it in his son's coffin, which he clutched until Cushing finally coaxed him away. "Come on, dear Jack, let's go," the cardinal said. "Death is not the end of it all, but the beginning." ■

CAROLINE HELD a postcard of her father in Hyannis Port. Opposite: John Jr. awaited his father's arrival at Camp David, the presidential retreat in Maryland, in 1963.

ESTATE OF STANLEY TRETICK LLC/CORBIS/GETTY (2)

ON OCTOBER 22, 1962, customers in a California store watched as Kennedy informed a worried nation about the Cuban missile crisis.

RALPH CRANE/LIFE/THE PICTURE COLLECTION

CHAPTER FIVE

THE CRISIS NEGOTIATOR

How JFK's political savvy helped avert a nuclear holocaust

"It is insane that two men... should be able to decide to bring an end to civilization."

—JOHN F. KENNEDY, ON THE POSSIBILITY OF NUCLEAR WAR, 1962

"IT SHALL be the policy of this nation to regard any nuclear missile launched from Cuba against any nation in the Western Hemisphere as an attack by the Soviet Union on the United States," Kennedy told the American public via television on October 22, 1962, adding that the United States would require "a full retaliatory response upon the Soviet Union."

The President was speaking against the Soviet buildup of nuclear missiles in Fidel Castro's Cuba. This was the time of the cold war, after all, and tensions between Russia and the United States were coming to a head.

Was Russia entirely the irrational, evil empire the public had been led to believe? "John F. Kennedy and his administration, without question, bore a substantial share of the responsibility for the onset of the Cuban missile crisis," according to Sheldon M. Stern, the John F. Kennedy library's historian for 22 years.

During his campaign, JFK had repeatedly perpetuated the concept of the "missile gap," falsely claiming that the Soviet Union had more ballistic weapons than the United States. Once in office, ostensibly trying to combat communism, Kennedy ordered the largest peacetime expansion of American military power and accelerated American aid to the South Vietnamese, deepening the nation's involvement in the disastrous Vietnam War. He established the Peace Corps in 1961, but even this admirable initiative—designed to aid people in developing countries—was a reaction against the Soviet Union, which, Kennedy said, "had hundreds of men and women, scientists, physicists, teachers, engineers, doctors, and nurses . . . prepared to spend their lives abroad in the service of world communism."

The Soviet threat was also approached in far more insidious ways. Designed to overthrow the Castro regime, the Bay of Pigs invasion was followed in November 1961 by the Department of Defense and the CIA's covert Operation Mongoose, a questionable plan run by Robert Kennedy, the President's brother and attorney general. "My idea is to stir things up on the island with espionage, sabotage, general disorder, run & operated by the Cubans themselves," he wrote in notes following a meeting with JFK and staff.

Some of Operation Mongoose's techniques were so bizarre they would have boggled James Bond, if not Austin Powers. The CIA considered using an exploding seashell or cigar to assassinate the dictator; deploying a depilatory to remove his distinctive beard; and dosing him with LSD. Astonishingly, the agency even hired the Mafia to eliminate the dictator, which J. Edgar Hoover's FBI discovered when its surveillance of Mob boss Sam Giancana revealed both the gangster's connection to the White House plot and the possibility that he shared a mistress with JFK.

In 1961, the United States began deploying Jupiter nuclear missiles in Italy and Turkey, directly threatening the Soviet Union. This was "a key reason for Khrushchev's decision to send nuclear missiles to Cuba," according to Philip Nash's *The Other Missiles of October*. The Soviet leader believed (accurately) that the United States was threatening his Cuban ally, Castro. Khrushchev wanted to prevent a potential "first strike" on the part of the United States.

The Kennedy administration had in fact discussed using nuclear arms

FIDEL CASTRO'S militiamen trained in Cuba's Escambray Mountains during the Cuban missile crisis.

HULTON-DEUTSCH COLLECTION/CORBIS/GETTY

CORNELL CAPA © INTERNATIONAL CENTER OF PHOTOGRAPHY/MAGNUM

against Russia during 1961's Berlin crisis, after the Soviet Union had demanded the removal of Western forces from West Berlin. Now, said Khrushchev, Americans "would learn just what it feels like to have enemy missiles pointing at you." Positioned just 90 miles from the Florida coast, the weapons would be, he said, "a little of their own medicine."

That's not how U.S. leaders saw it. "On Tuesday morning, October 16, 1962, shortly after nine o'clock, President Kennedy called and asked me to come to the White House," Bobby wrote in *Thirteen Days,* his memoir of the crisis. "He said only that we were facing great trouble. Shortly afterward, in his office, he told me that a U-2 had just finished a photographic mission and that the Intelligence Community had become convinced that Russia was placing missiles and atomic weapons in Cuba."

Two days later, JFK described the potential outcome of the standoff as "the final failure." Though most of the President's advisers recommended an air strike and invasion, Kennedy wisely argued for a more moderate approach. On the day of his press conference, he announced a quarantine—a blockade of Soviet ships—as military forces went to DEFCON 3 (a defense alert that goes from 5 to 1 in increasing severity). Later, they went to DEFCON 2.

The situation came to a perilous head on October 27, when an American pilot was shot down over Cuba and Soviet missiles were becoming operational. The President was being increasingly pressured to authorize an air strike. With the world on the brink of nuclear war, Khrushchev agreed to pull his missiles from Cuba—as long as the United States removed its own missiles from Italy and Turkey and publicly pledged to never invade Cuba. JFK agreed to the premiere's demands—with the stipulation that the removal of U.S. weapons from Italy and Turkey would not be revealed to the public. (The weapons' very existence was not officially disclosed until 1989.)

The crisis was finally over.

Despite JFK's early failings, he proved himself a levelheaded leader during a situation that, in lesser hands, could have led to Armageddon. "Once in the presidency there is virtually no

CONTINUED ON PAGE 74

ON OCTOBER 1, 1962, **Attorney General Robert F. Kennedy consulted with his brother (opposite) during the buildup of tensions between the United States and the Soviet Union. Above: Soviet premier Nikita Khrushchev and Kennedy in Vienna, 1961.**

AP

UNDERWOOD ARCHIVES/GETTY

A. Y. OWEN/THE LIFE IMAGES COLLECTION/GETTY

IN OKLAHOMA CITY, girls watched construction of a fallout shelter during the Cuban missile crisis, opposite.

Members of the antiwar group Women Strike for Peace (above) demonstrated near the United Nations in New York City, 1962.

CECIL STOUGHTON/CORBIS/GETTY

BETTMANN/GETTY

CONTINUED FROM PAGE 70

time for reeducation or the deep introspection that might show a President where he is right or wrong and bring about a true change of mind," wrote *Time* journalist Hugh Sidey in *Prelude to Leadership.* "Events move too fast. A President may pick up more knowledge about a subject or find an expert aide on whom he can rely, but in most instances when he is alone and faced with a crucial decision he must rely on his intuition, a mixture of natural intelligence, education, and experience."

Soon, tensions between the United States and the Soviet Union markedly decreased. A hotline was established between the Kremlin and the White House, and on August 5, 1963, the Limited Nuclear Test Ban Treaty was signed. But peace is, as JFK said, "the sum of many acts." As such, it is fragile. "Ever since the longbow, when man had developed new weapons and stockpiled them, somebody has come along and used them," the President told Sidey. "I don't know how we escape it with nuclear weapons." ■

PRESIDENT KENNEDY and General Maxwell D. Taylor visited Georgia's Fort Stewart on November 26, 1962, to thank the military for their service during the crisis (top). Bottom: On November 20, a clearly relieved JFK announced that the Soviet Union had agreed to remove bombers from Cuba and that the United States would lift its blockade. Opposite: A U.S. Navy patrol P3V-1 flew over a missile-carrying Soviet ship as it left Cuba.

CARL MYDANS/LIFE/THE PICTURE COLLECTION

150498
NAVY

NATIONAL GUARD soldiers escorted Freedom Riders from Montgomery, Alabama, to Jackson, Mississippi, in 1961. A group of civil rights activists, the Riders rode buses throughout the South to protest segregation at bus terminals.

BRUCE DAVIDSON/MAGNUM

CHAPTER SIX

THE CIVIL RIGHTS VISIONARY

With a single speech, Kennedy changed the nation's perspective on equality

The issue of civil rights "is as old as the scriptures and is as clear as the American Constitution."

—JOHN F. KENNEDY, IN AN ADDRESS TO THE NATION, JUNE 11, 1963

“THE UNWELCOMED, unwanted, unwarranted, and force-induced intrusion upon the campus of the University of Alabama today of the might of the central government offers a frightful example of the oppression of the rights, privileges, and sovereignty of this state by officers of the federal government.”

So said Alabama’s Democratic governor George C. Wallace on the blisteringly hot afternoon of June 11, 1963, as he blocked the doorway of the University of Alabama in Tuscaloosa, trying to prevent two black students, Vivian Malone and James Hood, from registering for classes. In what came to be known as the Stand in the Schoolhouse Door, Wallace was fulfilling—with deliberate drama—his inaugural promise of “segregation now, segregation tomorrow, segregation forever.”

John F. Kennedy had been elected at a time of racial strife unequaled since the days of the Civil War. Officials made it difficult for southern blacks to vote. Blacks couldn’t use “white only” drinking fountains or public facilities, were forced to ride in the back of buses, and were routinely subjected to both harassment and physical violence.

Some of this began to change—theoretically, at least—after the Supreme Court’s landmark 1954 *Brown v. Board of Education of Topeka* decision, which ruled that blacks should be allowed to attend previously segregated public colleges. Even so, threats and coercion kept many African Americans from pursuing education. In 1956, for instance, graduate student Autherine Lucy enrolled as the University of Alabama’s first black student, but she left a few days later, having been pelted with eggs, rocks, and bricks. She filed a complaint against the school, but withdrew it, and she was promptly expelled.

More than 70 percent of African Americans had voted for JFK, who had been a visible supporter of civil rights during his campaign (he helped secure the release of Martin Luther King Jr. from a Georgia prison after the activist was sentenced to hard labor for a mere traffic violation). After the election, concerned about alienating white southern voters, JFK refrained from taking an active stand on civil rights issues and instead avoided controversy by simply installing African Americans in the White House, while his brother Bobby focused on voting rights. But the President was soon forced to confront the larger issue head-on.

In September 1962, a riot consumed Oxford, Mississippi, after James Meredith, a black Air Force veteran, enrolled at the University of Mississippi. What followed was the “greatest insurrection in the South since Reconstruction,” according to journalist Andrew Cohen in *Two Days in June*. Two people were killed, leading Kennedy to rethink his moderate stance. “There comes a time,” he told an associate, “when a man has to take a stand and history will record that he has to meet these tough situations and ultimately make a decision.”

Kennedy’s characteristic pragmatism was also involved. “In a bipolar world ruled by the Soviets and the United States, the key to being powerful was to get the Third World countries to join your camp, and a lot of those leaders were black and brown,” says Barbara Perry. “It’s hard to make the case that you want them on your side in what Kennedy called ‘the great

PEACEFUL DEMONSTRATORS were slammed against a doorway by water from a fire hose, in Birmingham, Alabama, on May 3, 1963. The brutality of the local police brought national attention to the civil rights movement, spurring a previously hesitant Kennedy to support the cause.

CHARLES MOORE/GETTY

WASHINGTON
CONGRESS
OF
RACIAL
EQUALITY

CALVIN HANNAH/TUSCALOOSA NEWS/AP

UNIVERSAL HISTORY ARCHIVE/UIG/GETTY

twilight struggle' when you're treating your own minorities like second-class citizens."

Critics—including King—increasingly complained that the President was ducking the issue, but that would soon change. In May 1963, Eugene "Bull" Connor—an overzealous public safety commissioner in the Ku Klux Klan stronghold of Birmingham, Alabama—used dogs, clubs, fire hoses, and cattle prods to subdue more than 1,000 peaceful civil rights protesters, including women and children, led by King. The standoff ended only after coverage of the one-sided violence generated national condemnation, giving Kennedy an opportunity to take a stand. "Bull has probably done more for civil rights than anyone else," he said privately.

One month later, JFK had Wallace to deal with. Clearly relishing the publicity, the governor refused to relinquish his stance—literally—at the schoolhouse door, so Kennedy ordered the Alabama National Guard to remove him. Once he was gone, Hood and Malone calmly walked inside.

"Well," Kennedy said, "they got into the university."

That night, the President was scheduled to talk about the crisis on TV, but at 7:55 p.m.—five minutes before airtime—his speech was still being written by his chief scribe, Ted Sorensen. Three minutes later, the

ROBERT F. KENNEDY **(opposite) spoke on civil rights outside the Justice Department in June 1963. Top: On June 11, 1963, Alabama governor George C. Wallace (in doorway) blocked two black students from enrolling at the University of Alabama in Tuscaloosa. Bottom: After Wallace was removed, Vivian Malone entered the university's Foster Auditorium to register.**

WARREN K. LEFFLER/UNIVERSAL HISTORY ARCHIVE/GETTY

text was finally delivered to Kennedy in a confusing patchwork of fragments and pen marks.

"Thirty seconds," a technician said as the President settled in behind his desk, frantically scanning the text.

"Stand by, Mr. President."

Suddenly, Kennedy was live.

Speaking without a teleprompter and reading from the ragged notes, the President gave one of the most important speeches of his career, calling civil rights a legal, constitutional, and moral issue that "is as old as the scriptures and is as clear as the American Constitution." He said, "This nation was founded by men of many nations and backgrounds. It was founded on the principle that all men are created equal, and that the rights of every man are diminished when the rights of one man are threatened."

As Kennedy spoke, Sorensen kept writing, and pages were passed—unseen by viewers—under the desk. But for the final two minutes and 10 seconds of the speech, the President extemporized and spoke straight from the heart. "I am asking for your help in making it easier for us to move ahead," he said, "and to provide the kind of equality of treatment which we would want ourselves, to give a chance for every child to be educated to the limit of his talents."

The day's events marked the figurative end of segregation in the South. (Little more than two months later, hundreds of thousands of Americans watched Martin Luther King Jr. say "I have a dream . . ." during the March on Washington.) But JFK's concern that voters would turn against him proved well-founded: His approval rating dropped precipitously. The desire to reverse that drop was partly why, five months later, he went to Dallas. ■

ON JULY 11, 1963, the President addressed the nation in a speech that was written at the last minute. But Kennedy eventually ignored the text and improvised, speaking from the heart on live TV.

CORBIS/GETTY

ON AUGUST 28, 1963, civil rights leader Martin Luther King Jr. waved from the steps of the Lincoln Memorial in the March on Washington, during which he delivered his galvanizing "I Have a Dream" speech.

AFP/GETTY

CHAPTER SEVEN

THE LEGACY

An assassin took the life of a husband, a father, and a President, but JFK's words and deeds live on

"One brief shining moment."

—LYRICS FROM *CAMELOT*, THE 1960 MUSICAL THAT WAS A FAVORITE OF JFK'S

STAN STEARNS/BETTMANN/GETTY

THE IMAGE that broke a nation's collective heart: On his third birthday, John Jr. saluted as his father's casket was carried from the Cathedral of St. Matthew the Apostle in Washington, D.C.

26000.
U.S. AIR FORCE

"GOD, I HATE to go to Texas," Kennedy told a friend just before traveling to Dallas in November 1963. He was heading into what was then known as "the City of Hate"—a seething hotbed of racial and political tension—to generate support among divided voters and defuse conflict between Texas Democratic leaders. He hoped this would help pave the way to his reelection, but he had "a terrible feeling about going," he said.

Like Abraham Lincoln, Kennedy had long had premonitions of his own death, predicting that he wouldn't live past 45. (He was 46.) "Last night would have been a hell of a night to assassinate a President," JFK said on the morning of his assassination, according to William Manchester's *The Death of a President.* "I mean it. There was the rain, and the night, and we were all getting jostled. Suppose a man had a pistol in a briefcase." He made a shooting gesture with his hand. "Then he could have dropped the gun and the briefcase and melted away in the crowd."

Nevertheless, on the morning of November 22, 1963, the President insisted on riding in an open car—as long as it didn't rain, he said. "If the weather is clear and it's not raining, have that bubble top off," one aide told the Secret Service.

Dallas was the latest stop in a trip that had included visits to San Antonio and Houston. Leaving Love Field airport, the Kennedy motorcade headed down the 10-mile route to the Dallas Trade Mart, where the President was scheduled to speak at a luncheon. Around 12:30 p.m., as the motorcade passed the Texas School Book Depository and entered Dealey Plaza, shots rang out, one of them hitting Kennedy in the head.

Half an hour later, the President died at Parkland Memorial Hospital.

The shock and the outpouring of grief that followed were unprecedented. The first national tragedy widely covered by television, the assassination changed not only how the new medium operated but the way we collectively see things. In particular, the controversial Zapruder film of the assassination had a galvanic effect. Recorded by Dallas businessman Abraham Zapruder, the 8mm home movie captured the moment Kennedy was struck.

"The film quickly took hold of the public's imagination because it offered a shared vision of the tragedy that had befallen the young President and his wife," Alexandra Zapruder, the cameraman's granddaughter and author of *Twenty-Six Seconds,* tells LIFE. "The images preserved on the film became the nation's memory of the event—first in the form of still images in LIFE magazine and later in bootleg copies of the film that circulated around the country. At the same time, the film became the locus for all the complex and contradictory theories about what had actually occurred. Everyone, it seemed, saw something different when looking at the film, which eventually led to a rupture in the very idea of infallible visual records and the singular, unassailable truth they supposedly reflect."

During their Texas trip, the Kennedys were carrying an advance copy of *Look* magazine, which had a photo showing John Jr. peering from a small panel under the President's so-called *Resolute* desk. (The panel had been added to the desk to hide President Franklin D. Roosevelt's leg braces.) John Jr. called it "the secret door" to "my house." Released after

JFK AND THE FIRST LADY **arrived at Dallas's Love Field on November 22, 1963—the fateful day of the President's assassination.**

ART RICKERBY/LIFE/THE PICTURE COLLECTION

GEORGE F. MOBLEY/NATIONAL GEOGRAPHIC CREATIVE

the assassination, the image helped burnish JFK's legacy as a youthful family man tragically cut down in his prime. But another image of the boy would soon take an even more enduring place in history.

ON NOVEMBER 25, 1963, 70 photographers gathered at the Cathedral of St. Matthew the Apostle in Washington, D.C., covering Kennedy's funeral. Only one captured the moment when Jackie, draped in black, whispered in John Jr.'s ear, spurring the little boy, who was marking his third birthday, to salute his father's casket. "I asked every photographer I could if they had the salute," said UPI photographer Stan Stearns, the one who caught the shot. "Nobody saw it."

Even more moving, the moment was broadcast on TV. As such, it was part of Jackie's careful orchestration of the event, which she had patterned after Abraham Lincoln's funeral. "She looked at all the photos and drawings of that funeral that she could find," Barbara Perry says. "She started by festooning the White House in black crepe. Then there was the burial in military style with the riderless horse with the boots turned in reverse to indicate the fallen leader."

But it didn't end there. Less than a week later, trying to shape her husband's legacy before anyone else had the chance, Jackie gave an interview to LIFE journalist Theodore H. White. "At night, before we'd go to sleep," she said, "Jack liked to play some records; and the song he loved most came at the very end of this record. The lines he loved to hear were: 'Don't let it be forgot, that once there was a spot, for one brief shining moment that was known as Camelot.'"

Though JFK's reputation was eventually tarnished by revelations of womanizing, Mob connections, and espionage, Jackie had succeeded in establishing the exalted image of the President that prevails to this day.

NY DAILY NEWS ARCHIVE/GETTY

CAROLINE AND JACQUELINE said goodbye to JFK as his body lay in state (above) in the Capitol Rotunda on November 24, 1963. (John Jr. had gotten restless and was taken out.) Opposite, top: Commuters in New York City's Grand Central Terminal watched a broadcast of Kennedy's funeral. Opposite, bottom: Kohei Hanami, the Japanese naval commander responsible for sinking Kennedy's *PT 109* during World War II, watched news of the assassination in Tokyo.

ASAHI SHIMBUN/AP

TICKETS NEW YORK NEW HAVEN AND HARTFORD RAILROAD CO. TICKETS
SCHRAFFT'S
SAVE AT THE BOWERY

NASA/THE PICTURE COLLECTION, INC.

(Writing a tribute at Dallas's Sixth Floor Museum, one visitor called him "the greatest man since Jesus Christ.") Yet our culture is arguably more obsessed with youth than any civilization since the ancient Greeks, so we tend to enshrine and immortalize those whom "the gods" have taken from us in their prime, leaving them—and us—untainted by life's enduring disappointments.

JFK left an undeniably lasting legacy. His pioneering emphasis on the manipulation of image in politics has been adopted by every presidential candidate since—even though Kennedy's techniques have, as he himself had warned, often led to "manipulation, exploitation, and gimmicks."

On July 20, 1969, JFK's dream of an American walking on the moon before the end of the decade was realized when—after a four-day flight—*Apollo 11* astronauts Neil Armstrong and Edwin "Buzz" Aldrin set foot on the lunar surface. It was, Armstrong famously said, "one small step for a man, one giant leap for mankind." After exploring the surface for two and a half hours, the astronauts left behind an American flag and a plaque inscribed with the names of the astronauts and Kennedy's one-time rival Richard M. Nixon, then the U.S. President. Kennedy wasn't officially acknowledged, but not long afterward someone left flowers and a note on his grave: "Mr. President," it read, "the *Eagle* has landed."

Kennedy's adroit handling of the Cuban missile crisis paved the way for arms control negotiations and détente, according to Joseph Nye Jr. of the Harvard Kennedy School. Not least, said Nye, "if President Kennedy had not so deftly handled [it], we might not be here today to talk about it."

THE SECOND MAN to walk on the moon, Edwin "Buzz" Aldrin, stepped onto the lunar surface during *Apollo 11*'s historic landing on July 20, 1969—the fulfillment of JFK's goal of reaching the moon before the end of the decade.

ESTATE OF STANLEY TRETICK LLC/CORBIS/GETTY

In 1964, the Civil Rights Act ended public segregation and forbade discrimination on the basis of sex or race in hiring, promoting, and firing. It passed, thanks to the political maneuverings of President Lyndon Johnson. But it probably would not have been signed without the public's desire to honor the man who had first proposed it. Five days after the assassination, Johnson declared to a joint session of Congress that nothing would honor the slain President's legacy more. This impulse was also reflected in the passage of 1965's Voting Rights Act, which prohibits racial discrimination in voting practices. (In 2013, in a controversial five-four decision, the Supreme Court struck down a key provision of the law, holding that changes in civil rights meant it was no longer necessary.)

The battle for equality was hardly over, of course. Though both James Hood and Vivian Malone were allowed to enter the University of Alabama, Hood left on August 11, 1963, "to avoid a complete mental and physical breakdown," he said. (Someone had mailed him a dead black cat, and university officials tried to expel him.)

Malone, too, was harassed during the two years she spent at the university, but she graduated in 1965. Three decades later, George Wallace, the former Alabama governor who had blocked her from entering the university, honored her with the first annual Lurleen B. Wallace Award of Courage, named in memory of his late wife. The years had not been kind to Wallace—he suffered from Parkinson's disease and was crippled in an assassination attempt—but he had long since abandoned his segregationist stance and apologized, acknowledging that he had been wrong.

Now, as we celebrate the centenary of John F. Kennedy's birth, many of the issues he fought and even died for—civil rights, voting rights, nuclear disarmament—are under siege, but both the man and the myth endure in our collective memory. "The image of him that comes back to me," Theodore H. White wrote in his memoirs, "is so clean and graceful—almost as if I can still see him skip up the steps of his airplane in that half lope, and then turn, flinging out his arm in farewell to the crowd, before disappearing inside." ■

A NEWLY WIDOWED Jackie with her children in Hyannis Port, Massachusetts, in 1964 (above). Opposite: The Eternal Flame marks John F. Kennedy's resting place in Virginia's Arlington National Cemetery.

ROBERT F. SISSON/NATIONAL GEOGRAPHIC CREATIVE

JUST ONE MORE

PAUL SCHUTZER/LIFE/THE PICTURE COLLECTION

"CHANGE IS THE LAW of life," said JFK, shown here at the presidential inaugural ball in 1961. "And those who look only to the past or present are certain to miss the future."

19626989R00058

Printed in Poland
by Amazon Fulfillment
Poland Sp. z o.o., Wrocław